International Men's Day

The Birth of a Movement

I0438417

Jason Thompson

First published in December 2010
by Soul Books

Thompson, Jason. International Men's Day: The Birth
of a Movement

1st ed.

1. Masculinities. 2. Male Studies. 3. Global Events.

"Men respond more energetically to positive role models than to negative stereotyping."

CONTENTS

**International Men's Day gathering:
Sydney harbour, February 7th 1994**

Preface

The remarkable thing about International Men's Day is that it is inspired by a grassroots yearning, requiring little hard sell nor special marketing techniques. It has required no more than inviting individuals to celebrate all that is good about men and boys in order to garner their support, and to ensure ongoing momentum for the celebration.

My role has been to compile the event's history and to promote it more widely, on which basis I'm sometimes referred to as global promotions coordinator, and historian for IMD. However as a grassroots event with no management organization nor any hierarchy among participants I prefer to think of myself simply as an enthusiast, and in that spirit of enthusiasm I hope that International Men's Day continues to have a long and prosperous future, with this small volume being a contribution to that end.

Gathered here is a small selection of articles outlining the beginnings and purpose of International Men's Day. Some of the material has already been published online, and has been updated for this volume.

While detailing personal efforts to promote IMD, I do not wish to diminish the work of others who devoted an extraordinary amount of energy to promoting the event, both in individual countries and also globally.

On a strictly global scale there are three people that deserve a special tribute here - Professor Thomas Oaster who got the ball rolling, and later Dr. Jerome

Teelucksingh and Diane Sears who worked tirelessly to promote IMD, especially during the trailblazing days of 2007 – 2010, which saw come together an international 'coalition of the willing' to spread the word and promote the event, of which group I was a part. In the final days of 2010 I decided to compile this small volume to serve as a record for those wishing to study the beginnings of the event in future years.

Jason Thompson, June 2010

Introduction

International Men's Day (IMD) is an annual international event celebrated on 19 November. Inaugurated on February 7, 1992 by Professor Thomas Oaster, the project was re-initialised in 1999 in Trinidad and Tobago. The longest running celebration of International Men's Day is Malta, where events have occurred since February 7, 1994.

International Men's Day, now standardised globally as 19 November finds support from a variety of individuals and groups in Australia, the Caribbean, North America, Asia, Europe and Africa. Speaking on behalf of UNESCO, Director of Women and Culture of Peace Ingeborg Breines said of IMD, "This is an excellent idea and would give some gender balance." She added that UNESCO was looking forward to cooperating with the organizers.

Objectives of International Men's Day include a focus on men's and boy's health, promoting gender equality, and highlighting positive aspects of male experience. It is an occasion for men to highlight discrimination against them and to celebrate their achievements and contributions. November 19 is a significant date as it interfaces with campaign to stop violence against all people, the popular 'Movember' charity event and also with Universal Children's Day on Nov 20 with which IMD forms a 48 hour celebration of men and children respectively.

During the past ten years methods of commemorating International Men's Day have included public seminars, classroom activities at schools, radio and television programs, Church observances, and peaceful displays and marches. The manner of observing this annual day is optional; any organizations are welcome to host their own events and any appropriate forums can be used. Early pioneers of IMD reminded that the day is not intended to compete against International Woman's Day, but is for the purpose of highlighting men's experiences.

Each year secondary themes are suggested, such as peace in 2002, men's health in 2003, or Tackling society's tolerance of violence against men and boys in 2013, although it is not compulsory to adopt these themes and participants are welcome to come up with their own to suit local needs and concerns. In consultation with organizers from other nations IMD observes the following shared objectives which are applied equally to men and boys irrespective of their age, ability, social background, ethnicity, sexual orientation, gender identity, religious belief and relationship status:

■To promote positive male role models; not just movie stars and sports men but everyday, working class men who are living decent, honest lives.
■To celebrate men's positive contributions to society, community, family, relationships, child care, and to the environment.
■To focus on men's health and wellbeing; social,

emotional, physical.

■To highlight discrimination against males; in areas of social services, social attitudes and expectations, and law.

■To improve gender relations and promote gender equality.

■To create a safer, better world; where people can live free from harm and grow to reach their full potential

International Men's Day is celebrated in over 70 countries, including Trinidad and Tobago, Jamaica, Australia, India, Italy, United States, New Zealand, Brazil, Moldova, Haiti, St. Ketts and Nevis, Portugal, Singapore, Malta, South Africa, Ghana, Botswana, Angola, Zimbabwe, Croatia, Uganda, Chile, Hungary, Ireland, Peru, Canada, China, Vietnam, Pakistan, Denmark, Sweden, Norway, Guyana, Netherlands, Belgium, Georgia, Argentina, Mexico, Germany, Austria, Finland, Spain, France, and the United Kingdom. Join us on November 19 in celebrating men, along with the contributions make to those around them, to their family and friends, their work place and the community, the nations and the world.

Background

Calls for an International Men's Day have been noted since at least the 1960's when it was reported that "Many men have been agitating privately to make Feb 23 International Men's Day, the equivalent of March 8, which is International Women's day" (New York Times, Feb 24 1969).

Since that time there have been persistent international calls for the creation of an IMD, occasionally in the form of rhetorical questions – "Why do women have an international celebration and not men?" and more commonly in the form of statements like "Men's contributions and concerns deserve a day of recognition in their own right" i.e. not merely by analogy with International Women's Day.

Proposed objectives of an International Men's Day include a focus on men's and boy's health, improving gender relations, promoting gender equality, and highlighting positive male role models. It is also suggested as an occasion whereby men may highlight discrimination against them and celebrate their positive achievements and contributions.

In recent decades there have occurred a number of short-lived attempts at establishing an IMD in individual countries (eg. Canada, France, USA, Colombia, and Russia) with the hope that these gestures would be witnessed abroad by others who might follow suit and join in by celebrating their own IMD. Whilst small celebrations of this nature were apparently observed in a handful of countries, they suffered a lack of publicity necessary to reach interested parties abroad, and the initiatives were not continued.

In the early 1990s the first attempt to create a global IMD movement saw organizations in the United States, Europe, and Australia hold events in February at the invitation of Professor Thomas Oaster who directed the Missouri Center for Men's Studies at the University of Missouri–Kansas City. Oaster successfully promoted the event in 1993-1994, but his following attempt in 1995 was poorly attended and he ceased plans to continue the event in subsequent years. While the Australians also ceased to observe the event again until November 19, 2003, the original Maltese Association for Men's Rights continued to observe the event each year in February.

As the single remaining country still observing the earlier February celebration, the Maltese AMR Committee voted in 2009 to shift the date of their observation to November 19 in line with several countries that had come to celebrate on the newer date of November 19 which was promoted in Trinidad and Tobago by Dr. Jerome Teelucksingh in 1999.

The Caribbean initiated event grew slowly, but after the formation and work of the 2008-09 IMD steering Committee it received significantly increased support. Dr. Teelucksingh states, " My early efforts at observing and promoting International Men's Day were not successful. There was a disappointing public response as the first observances attracted only 5 to

10 persons. And, most of the times, members of my family comprised half the audience! The government and private businesses in my country were not interested in International Men's Day… . The steering committee of 2008 proved to be a powerful catalyst which contributed to the rapid spread of IMD."

The IMD Steering Committee of 2008 – 2009 consisted of five persons. This core group came together through casual discussions and all were eager to increase awareness about IMD and to foster it's growth into more nations. Perhaps the most significant achievement of the steering committee was to discuss and ratify six objectives of International Men's Day which would serve to protect the core values of the day and offer a reliable reference point for future celebrants. The 'six pillars' of IMD are:

1. To promote positive male role models; not just movie stars and sports men but everyday, working class men who are living decent, honest lives.
2. To celebrate men's positive contributions to society, community, family, marriage, child care, and to the environment
3. To focus on men's health and wellbeing; social, emotional, physical and spiritual.
4. To highlight discrimination against males; in areas of social services, social attitudes and expectations, and law
5. To improve gender relations and promote gender equality.
6. To create a safer, better world; where people can live free from harm and grow to reach their full potential.

Having achieved success in raising the profile of the event during those two years it was decided to dissolve the 'group of five' in favour of a more representative international group which would become known as the IMD Coordinators Network consisting of scores of individuals worldwide. The formation of the Coordinators Network List in 2010, whereby any persons could nominate themselves and be automatically placed on the list as a national or regional coordinator, ensured that the future of IMD was placed in the hands of the many, as opposed to a few, allowing the event to progress as a truly grassroots movement with no core management.

The one recommendation to new coordinators was that they agree to be guided by the six objectives of IMD (as above) and the official Diversity and Equality Statement

DIVERSITY AND EQUALITY STATEMENT

We encourage every man, woman, boy and girl in the world to join us in celebrating men and boys in all their diversity on International Men's Day (November 19th).

We recognize that there are a broad variety of laws, values and viewpoints around the world that affect different men, in different countries in different ways. There is also a diversity of opinions about those laws, values and viewpoints which are held by the many different men, women, boys and girls throughout the world.

As a day of observance we place our focus on that which unites humanity- giving everyone who wants to celebrate International Men's Day the opportunity to help work towards our shared objectives which we apply equally to men and boys irrespective of their age, ability, social background, ethnicity, sexuality, gender identity, religious belief and relationship status.

Due to the persistent networking and invitations sent to individuals in other nations International Men's Day has taken root on the international scene, and the initiative is now independently celebrated in countries as diverse as Singapore, Australia, India, Pakistan, United Kingdom, United States, South Africa, Haiti, Jamaica, Hungary, Malta, Georgia, Ghana, Moldova, Sweden, Norway, Denmark, Argentina, Brazil, Peru, Chile, Colombia, Spain, Wales, and Canada and interest in the event is increasing rapidly.

During the past ten years methods of commemorating International Men's Day have included public seminars, classroom activities at schools, radio and television programs, peaceful gatherings and marches, awards ceremonies, and art displays. The manner of observing this annual day is optional; any organizations are welcome to host their own events and any appropriate forums can be used.

Early pioneers of IMD reminded that the day is not intended to compete against International Woman's Day, but is for the purpose of highlighting *men's* experiences. Each year secondary themes are suggested, such as peace in 2002, men's health in

2003, or Tackling our tolerance of violence against men and boys in 2013, although it is not compulsory to adopt these themes and participants are welcome to come up with their own to suit their needs and local concerns.

Documenting International Men's Day

While IMD is presently a grassroots event it is rapidly becoming an organized global phenomenon, necessitating documentation of it's initial flourishing for those observing the event into the future. The following recounts an initial attempt at clarifying the early phase of the IMD movement, and the general intent of the event, whilst being aware that in writing such a 'narrative' I am laying a basis for future discussions.

I first became interested in International Men's Day after chancing upon a Wikipedia entry on the subject in 2007. This short account (see below) was the only attempt at a comprehensive statement to-date. After searching for more information I realized the Wikipedia entry presented some curious anomalies that didn't fit with the snippets of information I was reading elsewhere, such as the Wikipedia mention that Michael Gorbachev created the day –a claim bruted widely based on this mention– while other webpages mentioned Dr. Jerome Teelucksingh was the founder. As it turned out both Gorbachev and Teelucksingh were involved in different men's events, and neither was the founder of IMD – the true founder turned out to be an earlier worker in men's issues, Thomas Oaster.

The event that Gorbachev patronised was not a globally observed International Men's Day but an centralized Austrian awards event named 'Men's

World Day' which consisted primarily in a presentation ceremony to recognize men who have made a major contribution to society (the awards event has ceased to be observed as of 2006). The event which Dr. Teelucksingh promoted was the decentralised International Men's Day, observed annually in a variety of locations around the world on November 19. The facts about these two events had become conflated and needed disentangling. After reading more about the Austrian event I created a separate Wikipedia stub entitled Men's World Day and shifted all mention of the Gorbachev sponsored event to there.

A second error occurring in the Wikipedia article was a claim that IMD was already celebrated in numerous countries but on differing dates of the year. Nations cited as already celebrating the event included Poland and Slovenia (March 10), Norway (October 7), Hungary (May 19), Colombia (March 23) United Kingdom and Ireland (April 5), Canada (November 25), and Russia and Kyrgyzstan (February 23) and the Wikipedia article declared that these dates "have essentially become these countries' version of International Men's Day." This claim also turned out to be false because the above-mentioned countries were in fact celebrating unrelated traditions such as the Russian and Kyrgyzstan observation of 'Defender of the Fatherland Day'; in Hungary the 'Nameday of Ivó and Milán'; in Poland and Slovenia the 'Forty Martyrs of Sebaste'; and in Colombia, 'Saint Joseph Day'. Furthermore, it is doubtful whether there ever occurred events in the UK and Ireland on April 5, nor in Canada on November 25, which seemed more likely fanciful overtures betraying the wish to organise an IMD event rather than an actual record of events which took place.

To further complicate matters there appeared some confusion as to what exactly qualified as an 'International Men's Day' to begin with, with this title sometimes being applied to isolated/localised men's conferences to which international guests were invited. For instance, a men's conference held consecutively for 5 years in Ottawa during the late 1990's applied to itself the 'International Men's Day' title despite the fact it was not observed in any other international location. Such broad applications of the 'IMD' tag, if accepted as a standard definition, would have the effect of placing the first International Women's and Men's Days back thousands of years into history, there being numerous localized men's or women's gatherings throughout history with various foreigners in attendance.

Further, there are currently men's day celebrations which occur in one country on certain dates that are best qualified as National Men's Days despite the occasional use of the 'international' tag. A few national men's celebrations take place in countries like China on August 3, Brazil on July 15, Poland on September 30, Norway on November 8, and there are remnants of World Men's Day (Austria on Nov 3, and Russia on first Saturday in November) although there have been recently established in each of these countries celebrations of the International Men's Day on November 19. Time will tell if these national celebrations align more strongly with the internationally celebrated date or whether there will remain a comfortable coexistence of national and international days in those countries. With these "men's day" variations in mind I have chosen to limit the definition of International Men's Day to any continuous annual event observed in more than one country on an agreed date.

During the process of checking these facts it became apparent that important information was missing from the Wikipedia account, including mention that groups in other countries such as Australia, India, and Jamaica had previously joined in celebrating IMD with celebrants from Trinidad and Tobago since the year 1999. Moreover, there had been significant attempts at establishing IMD *prior* to the Caribbean attempt, such as the Kansas effort in the early 1990's which was taken up in some parts of the world.

Without any organized and accurate public record it was unlikely that the small, isolated celebrations that were then taking place would catch the attention of potential new participants. Also required by potential new IMD participants would be some knowledge that the event was not created nor controlled by radical fringe groups, and that it possessed social integrity worthy of organisational and individual endorsement. Both points suggested that only after gathering and publicly documenting all efforts into a coherent whole might then new organizations be inspired to join in. In hindsight this has certainly proven true, with a large increase in global awareness resulting from online publications and from the work of a handful of highly dedicated IMD coordinators.

As a grassroots movement IMD has suffered from a lack of recording, making it difficult for subsequent researchers to reconstruct a history. This book therefore is an attempt to document the main threads of IMD activity and while I have been diligent in gathering background material it is almost certain that undocumented efforts did occur which my searching did not unearth. For anyone wishing to investigate further, the folklore and written clues can be pursued to further add to our understanding of the fragments constituting the early movement.

Much material in the present account came to light through searches of the world wide web. When I was unable to complete a picture or needed more information I mailed key individuals whose names and contacts I was able to locate. The information offered herein represents only a portion of the historical account, albeit a significant portion, and while there may be occasional errors I have tried on the whole to adhere strictly to recorded information.

Popularizing International Men's Day

IMD is an occasion to promote positive male role models, celebrate men's positive contributions to the world, improve gender relations, promote gender equality, and to create a safer less-violent world. Of these Dr. Teelucksingh has laid importance on promoting positive male role models, "not just movie stars and sports men but everyday, working class men who are living decent, honest lives". The emphasis here is to remind that men and boys benefit by role models who can be emulated in everyday situations; at school, in the home, as parents, as workers, as partners and as friends, and not only as sports enthusiasts. Other possibilities afforded by IMD are the opportunities to highlight and redress gender inequality in areas of health, law and education, to redress unfair and narrow stereotyping of males, and to celebrate a variety of masculinities.

Having researched the beginnings of this event I became hooked by these and more wonderful possibilities for men, and with others continue to lobby international organizations and individuals to join the celebration. In the past some organisations had held localised men's days (eg. Maltese Association for Men's Rights on Feb 7; and POMESA and NAPWA of South Africa on Dec 6). After networking these organisations came to appreciate the advantages of joining a unified international movement to foster cooperation and solidarity. In 2008-09 I received commitments from various organizations in Europe, Africa, New Zealand and the Americas notifying of their intention to join November celebrations in 2009 and beyond. These gestures of solidarity would vastly increase exposure of IMD and rescue the event from public obscurity where it lay.

Popularizing IMD internationally was a relatively effortless task in the context of an increasingly negative global discourse about males elaborated over the last 40 years which has encouraged indiscriminate stereotyping, denigration of, and concomitant neglect of males in areas of education, health needs, social services and law, and also in their sense of social and personal wellbeing. Without that sense of wellbeing men and boys have been demonstrating a lowered motivation to contribute to the building of personal relationships or to the creation of healthy growing societies, this due to the distorted belief that any contributions would be unappreciated, and indeed unwelcome.

The path for many young men who have come to feel 'forced out' by negative stereotyping has been to 'drop out'. Many males have dropped out of school and society and dropped into drugs, gangs, violence, isolation, depression or suicide. Knowledge of this problem required no explanation to persons approached to participate in an International Men's Day -men and women from a wide variety of backgrounds, cultures and world views- as the problem had installed itself around the world and the majority of people were hungry for something, anything, which might turn the negative discourse around or at least balance that viewpoint with some needed positive discourse. The need to re-engage men and boys was obvious and IMD provided the platform from which to foster appreciation and encourage males back into participation with the world.

The idea of an International Men's Day was spreading, but due to language barriers IMD had not yet reached into nations of non-English speaking persons, necessitating translations of the IMD agenda which I undertook with the use of electronic translation technology or by commissioning others to translate into Spanish, German, French, Russian, Ukrainian, Portuguese, Finnish, Chinese, Vietnamese, Italian, Greek, Scandinavian languages, and so on. These translations were placed on Wikipedia and on various websites devoted to IMD, and then various individuals/organisations in each of these language centres were approached -translation of IMD objectives in hand- inviting them to participate.

Another, profitable approach was to trawl the web in search of individuals, in various countries, who had openly wondered if an IMD existed, or had otherwise proposed that one be established. By locating thousands of such mentions it was possible to email the individuals and start a conversation about the possibilities of joining IMD with some small or large observation. The resultant enthusiasm was remarkable and a significant number of those contacted pledged to immediately set about planning for an observation, and to spreading the word in their region. Again, once any firm observances were planned and convincing press releases were issued the various plans were published online.

The gradual expansion of an online repository, such as on Wikipedia, served as a significant encouragement to individuals who would soon make contact expressing their wish to observe the event, with ensuing discussions resulting in the formation of plans to celebrate. People who approached directly through the website came from a variety of countries including Mexico, Argentina, United Kingdom, Singapore, Austria, Pakistan, Grenada, Guyana, Zimbabwe, Mexico and others.

The strategy to encourage a relatively united event was deliberate, as the previous scattered voices calling for the establishment of IMD in different regions, on different days of the year, with different objectives, had become the subject of the all-too-common mockery of male initiatives: "men can't get their act together." Because of the lack of a singular annual date or set of objectives (not necessarily a bad thing!) few were taking it seriously.

Only by forming a united front with an agreed set of objectives and date might then the project be understood as a serious and legitimate undertaking. With the increasing legitimacy and respect being afforded to the event the current unity has achieved its aim. As it progresses the event will continue to encourage more flexibility in the timing and objectives of local observances to cater to local needs and concerns.

Thomas Oaster and Resistance to International Men's Day

This article is about how one gutsy MRA started International Men's Day despite attempts to shut him down. His name was Thomas Oaster.

Thomas Oaster was an articulate and passionate men's rights advocate. He was prolific in his work with men's groups, men's issues, and political advocacy both on and off campus where he taught. He had many fine MRAs around him, men and women who helped to improve the lot of males, but what of the man himself? Who was he really, and what is the unknown story of how he inaugurated the first International Men's Day? The following will be about Thomas Oaster and how he put IMD on the map for all who choose to celebrate the event into the distant future.

In the early 1990's Oaster's growing interest in advocating for men (and gynocentric resistance to that advocacy) led him to the idea of creating a globally celebrated International Men's Day. His goal was to create a platform where the stories of men could be told in their own words rather than being interpreted by others.

In a moment of nostalgia about this dream he mused:

> "You don't get points in men's groups for flexing your ego, but I'd like it to be known that Kansas City has become the hometown of

International Men's Day because a hometown boy got that thing rolling."[1]

As you will read in what follows Thomas Oaster, and Kansas City, can indeed now take credit for being the epicentre of a global movement.

The first IMD event took place in 1992 when small groups of MRAs scattered through 4 continents simultaneously celebrated with Oaster in the first celebration. Today, thanks to his vision, there are millions of people in more than 60 countries celebrating IMD. This achievement is remarkable when we consider it took place 20 years ago at a time when advocacy for men and boys was considered unthinkable.

Thomas Oaster was the Director of the Missouri Center for Men's Studies and employed as Associate Professor at the University of Missouri, Kansas City where he taught classes on men's issues. That's right, classes on *real* men's issues. He told of how he first became attracted to the men's movement by an intellectual interest, but quickly came to feel persecuted for his association with this politically incorrect subject. "I got beat up, slammed" reports Oaster, "People said, 'What – do you hate women?' The more I got beat up, the more I got drawn in. My Teutonic background took over." [1].

The first IMD event was launched on February 7, 1992 for the purpose of what he said was "drawing positive attention to important [men's] issues." [2] The event was successful both in 1992 and again in 1993 and 1994.[3] People in four continents celebrated and guests at the various events came along to hear speakers talk on topics ranging from the "silent tragedy of men's health" to "man bashing" and to share, talk, wine and dine.

It was a miraculous occasion. For the first time in history people gathered at the same time on four continents to actually speak of such things. On that day, February 7, men and women rejoiced in the company of like-minded souls as they shared intimate stories that ears had never before heard. Oaster spoke at his hometown Kansas event, reminding attendees that discussion of men's health and wellbeing deserved to be heard though the cacophony of misandry;

> "We want the bashing to stop. It's not a request. It's a statement. We want it to stop! To give you an example, a woman walked through here and saw the material and said, 'You've got to be kidding. You're not seriously going to have a men's day, are you?'"[4]

Oaster hoped that the day could become a means of education and consciousness raising where the positive cultural accomplishments of men could be celebrated and men might be faced with a better variety of choices about how they wanted to live their lives;

> "Women and men should both have options" wrote Oaster, and "International Men's Day is an opportunity to draw attention to the issue of options."[5]

Oaster proposed six core objectives for a men's day, and they were to: celebrate men's positive traits and contributions, improve gender relations, focus attention on men's health and wellbeing, remove misandry, increase life options for men and boys, and to develop a humanitarian-style approach to all men's issues. These six objectives were the foundations that would later be reaffirmed and ratified by a new generation of IMD celebrants, but not before a group of 'anti-Oaster' University women had played their final hand.

After the popular success of the first International Men's Day event in 1992, feminists at his campus became increasingly vindictive. During his planning for the 1994 and 1995 IMD events, a bomb was suddenly dropped by at least 6 former and current female 'graduate students' who collectively complained that Oaster had sexually harassed them and was "hostile" in the classroom.

The two most serious allegations put forward by the troupe were that Thomas Oaster had touched the forearm of one student with what she perceived was a "brief stroking motion", and that he had advised another student to dye her hair blonde in response to her question about what she could do improve her poor grade. To drive the nail deeper another student said he had referred to her as "Blondie" at least twice. The curators at the university entertained these shallow and dubious allegations and were quick to respond by imposing restrictions on Oaster's movements and work. [6]

Despite these distractions the next two IMD events went extremely well with several hundred individuals in attendance. However the fourth year of IMD heralded a change in the weather when his antagonists decided to double-down in their efforts to shut him down.

In 1995 Oaster had planned to orchestrate his fourth and biggest IMD event when he increasingly became the target of workplace bullying. He decided to sue the Curators of the University for Infringement of his civil rights as a tenured professor, claiming that he was being denied freedom of speech, salary increases, graduate teaching assistants and the use of university facilities.[6] Naturally the court proceedings took up much of his time and energy and this taxed his ability to effectively organize or advertise the upcoming IMD event.

Due to these circumstances the next IMD event was a flop with few people turning up. After this failure, and feeling drained by a complex court case, Oaster decided to defer future IMD plans and take a well-deserved rest.

With precision, Thomas Oaster had been persecuted for his role in the men's rights movement. [6] Late in 1995 Oaster won his court case against the UMKC and the University was forced to pay him $74,000 plus $15,000 for legal fees. After settlement Oaster resigned from his job as he felt he would no longer have the respect of his students, and he shelved plans to continue celebrating IMD. [6]

General interest in the event waned until 1999 when Dr. Jerome Teelucksingh, a History Professor at the University of the West Indies revived the event and shifted the date to November 19 – the date of his father's birthday.

Jerome Teelucksingh continued Oaster's emphasis on highlighting positive aspects and accomplishments of men. In a 2009 interview Teelucksingh also gave a nod to the work of Oaster when he stated this;

> "I could be considered the founder of this version of IMD on 19 November *but we need to also acknowledge the pioneering efforts of persons and groups before 1999… They are the ones to be honoured."* [3]

In 2009 an international IMD committee was formed with Jerome Teelucksingh as chairman. The group came together to increase awareness about the event and to foster its growth into more nations.

Taking note of the foundational IMD objectives introduced by both Oaster and Teelucksingh, the committee encapsulated the objectives of International Men's Day in six guiding principles that would serve to protect the core values of the day and offer a reliable reference point for future IMD celebrants.[3] The 'Six Pillars,' which are suitably loose and open to interpretation, are now used as a guide by IMD celebrants around the world:

- To promote positive male role models; not just movie stars and sports men but everyday, working class men who are living decent, honest lives.

- To celebrate men's positive contributions to society, community, family, marriage, child care, and to the environment.
- To focus on men's health and wellbeing; social, emotional, physical and spiritual.
- To highlight discrimination against males; in areas of social services, social attitudes and expectations, and law.
- To improve gender relations and promote gender equality.
- To create a safer, better world; where people can live free from harm and grow to reach their full potential

It's my belief that the spirit of Oaster's original vision and that of contemporary male human rights website A Voice for Men (AVfM) have much in common. Both movements aim to create an inclusive international voice for men as free as possible from sectarian ideology. Moreover, both IMD and AVfM reject the notion of a unified men's movement, encouraging instead a diversity of men's voices on a variety of humanitarian issues:

Thomas Oaster said this:

> [T]here is no such thing as a unified men's movement, the phenomena involved comprise a variety of sub-movements, even after analogies to other issues concerning which there are far left, far right, and middle-of-the-road orientations, there is yet another more

fundamental point which can be made about the value of respect for all men as human beings. A day of respect should go beyond the current social activities referred to as Men's movements. This is true because the men's movement itself goes beyond the Men's movements. The men's movement, more fundamentally, is a turning of the human psyche and the articulation of this turning through the male voice.[5]

Paul Elam, founder of <u>avoiceformen.com</u> said:

[C]ontinuing to buy into the false unity of a non-existent entity will only slow us down. I have always taken care, and still do, to point out that AVfM is not synonymous with the men's movement. And after mulling this over one more time of thousands, I am really glad that I have taken this approach. I don't know what the men's movement is, in all honesty. I don't even know that it exists.[7]

While the similarities in the two movements are obvious, there are some important differences. For instance in Thomas Oaster's day there was no internet, whereas today it is a vital medium for all activism, including on the AVfM platform. Another difference is that IMD focuses the year-long work of activists into one big day of publicity, whereas other activists strive to make 'every day' a men's day via regular online publicity.

International Men's Day is a grassroots movement with no official management. It does not belong to any government nor is it owned by the United Nations or any of its agencies. We might say that nobody owns the event, or better yet *everybody owns it*. Any person can self-nominate as an IMD coordinator for a specific region or event and, if desired can form alliances with an international network of individuals working to promote the day. Any current and future coordinators are merely hitch-hikers catching a ride on an international platform that nobody owns.

Nobody needs to gain permission to mark the day. All one need do is be mindful of the spirit of the occasion as laid out in the six pillars which ask us to remain true to the lives of men and boys without allowing that message to be diminished by negative or irrelevant concerns.

In recent years IMD has spread into new regions and attracted some mainstream attention. With this new attention it is perhaps time to remind newcomers that the originators of the event were fighting for liberty and freedom, and that we still have a very long way to go on this front.

With this in mind let us finish with words of Abraham Lincoln's Gettysburg address, itself delivered on November 19- the date of International Men's Day. The words of his address speak equally to the purpose of International Men's Day today and of the great sacrifices made by Oaster and other men and women who fought on the battlefield of cultural misandry;

> 'Four score and seven years ago our fathers brought forth on this continent, a new nation,

conceived in Liberty, and dedicated to the proposition that all men are created equal. Now we are engaged in a great civil war, testing whether that nation, or any nation so conceived and so dedicated, can long endure... The brave men, living and dead, who struggled here, have consecrated [the ground], far above our poor power to add or detract. The world will little note, nor long remember what we say here, but it can never forget what they did here. It is for us the living, rather, to be dedicated here to the unfinished work which they who fought here have thus far so nobly advanced.' [Lincoln]

Despite the resistance, the tradition of IMD lives on. In Oaster's name let's dream it forward.

Sources

[1] George Gurley, 'Finally, men get their day' (Kansas City Star: Feb 6, 1993)
[2] Fred Wickman, 'about Town' (Kansas City Star: Jan 27, 1992)
[3] Jason Thompson, 'International Men's Day; the making of a movement' (Soul Books, 2010)
[4] James Fussell, 'Men have their say at weekend forum' (Kansas City Star: Feb 6, 1993)
[5] Thomas Oaster, 'International Men's Day: RSVP' (Cummings and Hathaway, 1992)
[6] Cheryl Thompson, 'Complaints surface about UMKC professor' (Kansas City Star: Mar 10, 2003)
[7] Paul Elam, 'Adios, c-ya, good-bye man-o-sphere' (A Voice for Men. retrieved October 2012)

Origins and Evolution; Perspectives of International Women's and Men's Days

International Men's and Women's days involve numerous objectives, with both days highlighting issues considered unique to men or women. The following highlights two central currents of IWD and IMD respectively; women's supposed fight against oppression, and men's attempts to promote positive recognition of men and boys in a misandric society.

Several popular myths concerning the origins of International Women's Day exist, and after a survey of the literature it seems the variety of accounts have created confusion for commentators. For example, a widely bruited falsehood about IWD which surfaced in French Communist circles claimed women from clothing and textile factories had staged a protest on 8 March 1857 in New York City.

This story alleged that garment workers protested against very poor working conditions and low wages and were attacked and dispersed by police. It was claimed that this event led to a rally in commemoration of its fiftieth anniversary (in 1907), with this commemorative gathering constituting the very first IWD. In response to these legendary claims Temma Kaplan explains that "Neither event seems to have taken place, but many Europeans think March 8, 1907 inaugurated International Women's Day."[1]

This fantasy of origins clearly attempts to position International Woman's Day in a narrative of woman-as-victim, but it goes further. Speculating about the origins of the 1857 legend Liliane Kandel and Françoise Picq suggested it was likely that some felt it opportune to detach International Women's Day from its basis in Soviet history and ascribe to it a more 'international' origin which could be painted as more ancient than Bolshevism and more spontaneous than a decision of Congress or the initiative of those women affiliated to The Party.[2]

Whilst numerous apocryphal stories of this nature exist, we can safely say that International Women's Day was first initiated by German socialist Clara Zetkin in 1910 as a way to promote socialist political objectives and was always referred to by the political name 'International Working Women's Day'. Observation of the event was primarily restricted to the Soviet bloc. It wasn't until the 1970s when women outside of the Soviet bloc looked to celebrating the event that the word 'working' was increasingly omitted along with much of its socialist meaning.

Beginning in the 1970's IWD became subject to a feminist revision. Whereas IWWD was previously used to highlight working women's oppression by a bourgeois and powerful upper class of both men and women, 1970s feminists revisioned the basis of the day by stating that it was now men alone, as a class of "chauvinists," who wielded all power over all women who had each become victims of men's domination. It was men's oppressive rule which IWD must now focus on overthrowing.

A decisive moment of the feminist revision came from the United Nations which officially endorsed and promoted the event from the late 1970s. Along with this endorsement the UN worked very hard to get rid of IWDs socialist traits, a move which was not accepted by many socialist women's groups. For instance, in 1980 in Sweden, the socialist women's 'Grupp 8' rejected working with other women's organizations to promote IWD because it wanted to maintain the socialist origins and aims of the event: "We have now conducted a number of discussions within our organization and come to the conclusion that, as representatives of the socialist women's movement, we cannot take part in a joint-party March 8 demonstration. After all, from the historical perspective, March 8 is the 'International Socialist Working Women's Day' and our organization feels that this should absolutely remain the case. Changing this would be like changing May 1. For this reason we are unable to endorse the UNs appeal."[3] The revisioned event was seen by many as a betrayal of both its history and fundamental goals.

A popular slogan circulated on International Women's Day on posters, pin-buttons, T-shirts, bumper stickers, and in print media.

With this new ideological turn women were no longer viewed as part of the privileged upper class, and those former oppressors of women- i.e. capitalism; traditional gender schemas imposed by powerful men and women; various laws, language and so on- were reduced to one all-encompassing enemy: males and their patriarchal belief system. The new ideological basis for IWD was elaborated in the late 1970s-80s under the label "patriarchy theory"[4] and its arrival correlated with a sharp increase in the numbers of women observing IWD,[5] an interest generated by heightened concerns or fears over 'patriarchal oppression' of women.

It's true that women have sought to dismantle restrictive gender stereotypes, but IWD appears more concerned with *perpetuating* those gender stereotypes rather than dismantling them. In light of the oversimplified explanations proposed by feminist 'patriarchy theory'[6] one hopes that whatever issues remain for women that they be explored in more sophisticated and nuanced ways to give International Women's Day a more credible platform for promoting gender equality and improving gender relations.

International Men's Day, as conceived by Professor Thomas Oaster in 1992, and Dr. Jerome Teelucksingh in 1999, has a completely different ideological basis to both the early and later phases of International Women's Day. Although the objectives of IMD occasionally intersect with those of IWD, such as advocating equality between the sexes, it is primarily concerned with celebrating *positive* portrayals of men and other issues unique to men's and boys' experiences.

This approach is deemed necessary in a social context which is often fascinated with images of males behaving badly, eg. media portrayals of males as stupid, emotionless, greedy, violent, dangerous, power-hungry, selfish, irresponsible and so on. Such negative male stereotypes are frequently promoted in an attempt to shame males into behaving more positively, ignoring the fact that the negative behaviours do not apply to the vast majority of men and boys, or that such negativity may detrimentally impact the self-image and self-esteem of boys, which in turn impacts their willingness to engage in intimate relationships and in communities. In highlighting positive images of men IMD attempts to show that males of all ages respond more energetically to positive portrayals than they do to negative stereotyping.

In summary, International Women's Day started as a day for women to promote socialist objectives, especially for proletarian women to fight against oppression by the powerful upper classes comprised of *men and women both*. In the 1970's it became a new movement claiming that men alone oppressed women, and that IWD will be used as a vehicle to highlight, primarily, the results of an assumed gender war. Said differently the focus of IWD shifted from a class war, to a gender war.

International Men's Day is not based on the assumption of a gender war. IMD is primarily about celebrating positive images of men as an alternative to negative male stereotyping, the aim being to inspire a new generation of men and boys to develop self-worth and a desire to participate in a society that will (hopefully) one day be free from misandry.

References:

[1] Temma Kaplan, On the Socialist Origins of International Women's Day, in: Feminist Studies, 11, 1985, S. 163-171.
[2] Liliane Kandel / Françoise Picq, Le Mythe des origines à propos de la journée internationale des femmes, in: La Revue d'en face, 12, 1982, S. 67-80.
[3] Silke Neunsinger, Worlds Of Women; International Material in the Collections of ARAB, p23 – letter by Grupp 8, Stockholm, 1981
[4] Lindsey German, Theories of Patriarchy in International Socialism second series no 12. 1981.

[5] 1900-2010: Increased interest in IWD correlates with the emergence of 'patriarchy theory'.

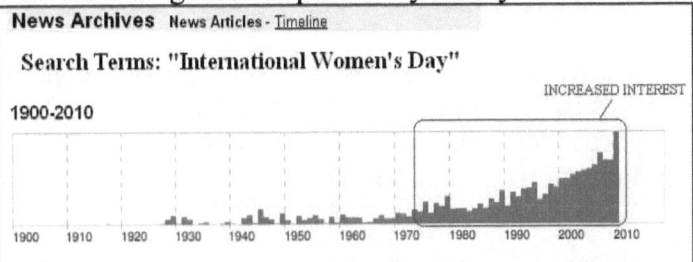

In the early 1970s feminists developed a new terminology. Just as blacks were oppressed by "racism", oppressive attitudes toward women needed a name. The early activists hit upon "male chauvinism". A few years later a new word appeared "patriarchy". But this was not just a new term for women's oppression. It reflected claims by feminists to have discovered a new system of social structures: a "patriarchal" system in which men as a group ran the world. The news article timelines below show a correlation between increased interest in International Women's Day and the promotion of the words "chauvinism" and "patriarchy" respectively.

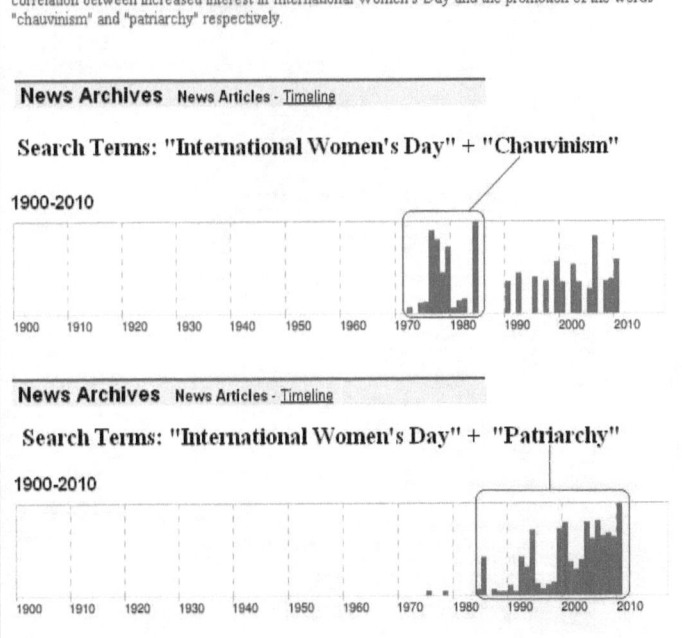

Historical Timeline

The timeline below represents a snapshot of the main strands of IMD to the year 2010. Since that time IMD has expanded into more than 70 countries and participation continues to grow.

TIMELINE

1965 — VARIOUS CALL FOR IMD

1992 — KANSAS STREAM - FEBRUARY 7th

U.S.A. | CANADA | FRANCE | BRITAIN | AUSTRALIA | MALTA

DISCONTINUED 1995

1999 — CARIBBEAN STREAM - NOVEMBER 19TH

CARIBBEAN | AUSTRALIA | INDIA | U.K. | SINGAPORE

Trinidad & Tobago	- 1998
Jamaica	- 2001
Australia	- 2003
Barbados	- 2004
Haiti	- 2005
India	- 2007
Singapore	- 2008
United Kingdom	- 2008

IMD Global Website created - 2007

2008 — SOUTH AFRICA - DECEMBER 6th

Malta and South Africa shift their IMD dates to November 19 - 2009, creating a single united world movement.

2009 — Malta, South Africa, United States, Netherlands, Canada, Hungary, Ghana, Georgia, Ireland, Italy — Joined

2010 — Numerous organizations/individuals join to celebrate: IMD events held in 41 countries — Joined

Timeline - by Jason Thompson